The Plumber's Apprentice

Also by Joe Weil

Painting the Christmas Trees, Texas Review Press, 2008

What Remains, Nightshade Press, 2008

The Plumber's Apprentice

Joe Weil

The New York Quarterly Foundation, Inc.
New York, New York

NYQ Books™ is an imprint of The New York Quarterly Foundation, Inc.

The New York Quarterly Foundation, Inc.
P. O. Box 2015
Old Chelsea Station
New York, NY 10113

www.nyqbooks.org

First Edition

Set in New Baskerville

Layout and Design by Raymond P. Hammond
Cover Illustration: "French Press," oil on pizza box, by Jamie DeAngelo, 2009
Cover Design by Natalie Sousa
Frame/Background photo © Hardtmuth used under license from Shutterstock.com

Library of Congress Control Number: 2009937039

ISBN: 978-1-935520-10-8

The Plumber's Apprentice

Acknowledgments

Grateful Acknowledgements are made to the editors of the following publications, in which some of the poems in this collection first appeared or are forthcoming: *Arbella, Arc of A Cry, Cartographer Electric. Big Hammer, The Idiom, Lips, Louisiana Review of Literature, Journal of New Jersey Poets, Paterson Literary Review, The New York Times, The Star Ledger,* and *Ragzine,* an online journal. Some of the poems appeared earlier in an online chap book published by Cartographer Electric called *Teaching The Dead,* and "At The Camden Aquarium" is included in an upcoming anthology of poems from New Jersey.

Mr. Weil would also like to express his gratitude to Micah Towery, Dana Jaye Cadman, and Tom Bair, former students who have been of major help to him in gathering his scattered and sprawling work over the past two years. I dedicate the book to Leslie Heywood, but her friendship and organization of my manuscripts are beyond anything a dedication can render. She has opened the doors to her family during a time in my life when all sense of family was lost. For Leslie, her husband Barry, and their daughters, Caelan and Keene.

For Maria Gillan, Leslie Heywood, and the Neighborhood:

Survival

Contents

II. How Holy

III. It's Like This

"Now this field…"

I. There Goes the Neighborhood

Christmas, 1977

Here where it is always Bethlehem,
grimy, grieved—a slum lord's kind of town,
I watch old Mrs. Suarez string her lights
against the common vespers of despair.

I watch her nimbly snub the cold night's air,
thwarting a fall into the snow ball bush
beside which Mary calmly stomps the skull
of Satan. Look! the Lights are coming on:

Blue with white specks, where the paint has chipped,
and yellow, green, all rising to full glow,
big gum drop lights, draped from post to post,
haloed where their heat meets with the cold.

And something in me tears or has been torn
a long, long time, though I have read Rimbaud,
and have been known to chew on my own spleen,
and spend an evening jesting at a God.

Something in me breaks and will not mend,
Take up my broken hymn and sing it there
for Mrs. Saurez, wobbly, and infirm,
who soon will be too old to climb her chair.

For her I hang this broken Christmas hymn,
here, where it is always Bethlehem.

In the Camden Aquarium

A woman in a light green dress
with matching hand bag,
an expert on Dante who,
taking off her white gloves,
with a careful, careful nonchalance,
sits down to read the
Vita Nuova:

I hear her as I stand
watching the fish swim
in the Camden aquarium.

Camden: gutted city
where still the sound of Italian vowels
and the silence of fish recall

I am human. I am
falling to my death. I
am falling
deathwards, but at this
voice full of Dante
who has time to gauge the height?

So each beautiful thing is reprieve,
and stay of execution,
recompense

the face of a child
the color of apricots
so close against the glass
his fingers smudge the fish—

his mother yanks his arm,
the fish escape—
languid tails disappearing
into the dark,
one final glint of a scale—
that flashes silver, one full Italian vowel.

When I Was Twelve

When I was twelve, I spent a year staring at the back
of Maria Casarez's head, all through
history, and religion, and Math, and I never grew bored.

All my friends preferred Patty Low—the blonde with the periwinkle eyes,
and I had nothing against blondes, with periwinkle eyes,
but I wrote my first poem for Maria:

I wrote that her hair was a dark lawn at dusk,
on which old men and women played croquet,
that she was sad and wonderful—like a finger nail moon above
Blumetti's Liquors.

I read a poem in a book I stole from the library.
(Books were always better when you stole them)
It read: "Lark of my house, laugh often."

It was by the Spanish poet, Miguel Hernandez,
tubercular Shepard, whom Franco had locked up in prison.
The introduction was by Pablo Neruda.

I knew nothing of Pablo Neruda or Miguel Hernandez,
knew nothing of poetry except that Hernandez's wife and son
had been starving, living on little but wild onions,

and that, from his prison cell, from his dying,
he wrote: Lark of my house laugh often,
so that, even dead, and whirling through space,

I might hear your laughter,
Lark of my house, laugh often and grow strong,
for you can eat the moon when you want to."

These words made me cry. I walked home past the basketball courts,
past St. Mary's cemetery, past the billboard of the Marlboro man,
and decided I was in love with Maria Casarez.

Love made me feel enormous, and frightened,
and so small all at once,
and now I knew why idiots broke into song,

in the middle of movies, why they swung from light poles,
and tap danced on ceilings. I wanted to die for something—
or live in this intensity that had overwhelmed me so that

I suddenly noticed the stars hung in the anemic swamp maple
outside my frame house, so that this tree was now
the heaven tree of stars, and not just the pain in the ass

my father wanted to cut down,
so that now I was ready to read poems, and to live and die,
as the Lark of somebody's house.

A Typical Day 31 Years Ago

was watching my mother die.
Part of the tumor that would
eventually strangle her
came out of her mouth
like a cheap party trick,
just in time for the feast
of the epiphany.

She thought it was a good thing
a sign radium and chemo,
were finally hitting their stride,
breaking things up,
as if her cancer were a vaudeville circuit.

She was wrong. We were all wrong.
I danced for her anyway, did my
best routines, told the only
pretty girl in high school who ever phoned me
that I couldn't talk right then,
and when she showed up at my house
anyway, radiant, with a Bundt cake
from her mother
to mine,
she caught me in the act
of lying to that hairless woman
with the three inch hole in her face ,
telling her they'd replace
the jaw bone
soon, and she'd go to Ireland, soon
and the beautiful hair would all grow back,
soon.

I've been lying all my life.
It's so easy. You just pull out
all the truths God so
generously bestows
and draw a smiley face.
You say soon. It is always soon.
It's been soon for thirty years.
You remember
you are not the one who is
crying in pain, but you are,
and that's a lie. Yes. And that's
the truth, and the pretty girl
leaves the Bundt cake
and flees, and doesn't take your calls
ever again
and you are 49,
and your girlfriend
envies you because you're not the one
screaming in pain, but you are,
and that's a lie, yes, and that's
the truth. You have always been
so alive, and people have hated you
for it—but buried alive.
You are sick of vaudeville. Didn't it die?
People like when you dance,
juggle your balls, take the pie
in the round and jowly face.
Tell them to fuck off,
tell the girls with the Bundt cakes
to fuck off. They just wanted
to drop things off from a better place,

to let you know what you're missing.
Be alone with the one who is always dying—
hey, that's you!
You've been dying for thirty-one years.
When you told your mother
you wished it was you, she said,
"I know you do and that's what scares me."
You always mean it.
Even when you lie, you mean it,
with your whole heart, you would do
anything
to take it away, to own it yourself,
but you don't, and it comes back, and comes back
and it always wants to play,
always. Here, take this ball.
Fetch.

For Jordan, a Kid from Paterson Who Visited My House

We cart rocks from the flood wall
to surround the fire,
great heaving stones that make dents in the soft earth.

These kids from a neighborhood of street gangs
are afraid of the daddy long legs in the shower.

I swat and smush casually with my hand,
killing all bugs, showing off for the boys.

We sit down by the fire, telling ghost stories,
bragging and laughing, risk getting burned

leaping over the flames. I haven't felt
this alive in years. The older brother, Jordan,
remembers his father, a dealer who got busted

and sent up for 13 years. I say to him:
"He must've been top of the line.

Thirteen years…shit, that ain't no punk time."
He nods: "Yeah, we had a big house—three floors"
and takes a stick to the hot coals and scrapes

until they burst into flame. He tells me his dad
smiled when he visited him in prison. His father's

getting deported to Columbia as soon as
his stretch is up. He wants to see his father again, there,
on the coast, where they ride white horses

through the foam of the sea, where every rock
has a story. His dark eyes stare at me through the flames.

There are tears massing at the borders of his eyes.
He is looking for a father anywhere. Me, too.
How fragile our bravado is. I teach him how to

bob and weave, how to cut the ring, throw
from the heel. No round house. He wants to be a boxer
and a writer. When I give him my poems,
he reads them through, long and carefully.
says with surprise "You don't write like a white guy."

This is my highest compliment. I know, I tell him
in my neighborhood the Cuban Grandmas

called me *El Blanco*. He picks up a marshmallow
the last one, and offers it to his little brother.
He has valor, a good heart. What will these do for him?

A single beef, and he might catch a bullet.
The world is not particular in whom it chooses

to slaughter. His father, he says, was different.
He read books. He sang songs. He dealt dope
because he wanted that house with three floors

and no roaches—bug free, a clean shower.
When they go, the land seems to hold them

a few hours, the way a pool empty at dusk
holds the afternoon's laughter, the sounds of
splashing, the voices of kids horsing around

until the dark drops down to silence it again.
I clean out the ash from the fire. I, too,

am an orphan upon the earth. *El Blanco,* the whitest
motherfucker in my neighborhood.
I say a prayer for him. I pray he gets those

hooves in the foam of the sea. I pray
he dodges every bullet. What the fuck?

What can a man do with a land where
every stone tells a story? Listen. Shemah
lost in the busy lives we think we lead—

the mute essential poverty,
the true blood of stones and stars.

Remember When I Loved You Enough to Listen to Neil Diamond Singing Cracklin' Rosey

Remember, you were a rabid Neil Diamond fan,
and this was unforgivable,
especially since it preceded the
Brave New World of campy cool.
I lay on your water bed, literally sea sick,
amid your six Abbysinian cats
to which I was allergic,
in an overly air conditioned room,
where they purred in unison,
as if to curse our love,
and I was happy.
Yes, even with my eyes puffed up,
even with my breathing greatly impeded,
I awaited your return from the bathroom,
freezing, my nipples turned to granite rose buds,
my penis half-mast,
and Neil sang:
"Rosey, you're a store bought womun
but you make me sing like a gee-tar hummin,"
and I thought: Shit, I finally know,
love transcends aesthetics, as I lay there
spread on the wrack of that wobbling rectangle—
the hangman, the sacrifice of the mass,
and when you crawled into bed,
the Abyssinians uncoiling and purring
with far greater vehemence between your naked limbs,
you said: I love Neil Diamond.
And I said: Me, too,
telling the greatest and most pernicious lie of my life,
amid all my great and pernicious lies,
and you finally shooed the cats away,
and we fucked, and fucked,

though the bed kept shifting beneath our weight,
and the silk sheets made me slide,
after which, I said: I have something to tell you.
You said: What babe?
I said: Neil Diamond makes me puke.
And I put on my pants, and belt, etc, etc,
fleeing my falsehood, knowing it would be hard
to return, fearing God would send me to that hell
for men who lie to get a piece of ass,
that place where Neil sings: I am said I
for all eternity, as the record skips,
and the Abyssinians purr.

In My Neighborhood Everyone Almost Wins the Lottery

There was Mrs. Spazzola who dreamed
the moon was following her late beloved husband,
Patsy Spazzola,
on his way to his old job,
the one he'd lost before the tumor showed
and finished him off,
and she tried desperately to remember
the exact address of his old factory,
but got it wrong, and—wouldn't you know?
That was the pick five number that paid a hundred thou.

And there was Jimmy the horse, the bookie
with the sizable overbite
who, rumor had it, had won but kept
the million cash pay out
under his bed which he set on fire
drunk on Johnny Walker Blue.

When the fire went out, all that was left of Jimmy
were his gold plated cuff links, and a couple of teeth.

All around my neighborhood's misery,
the right combinations hover, dance,
whisper into ears of otherwise
devout members of the Holy Name.

When the pot's really big, Maya gives out
free coffee at Lew's Luncheonette. The Botanica
can't keep the African gods/saints candles in stock.
It's up to 80 mill, somebody says, half whispering.
I don't need that much.

SHHHHHHHIIIIIIIIIIIIITTTTTT, emits wino Pete
don't jinx me with that modest shit. I'll take
whatever them motherfuckers give.

No one ever wins. Everyone knows someone
who would have won, if only they had followed
their hearts, or remembered an address, or
been born on a lucky day.

For awhile, the block turns lively, almost festive,
then sinks back into its perpetual decay—
cancer, lay offs, ancient rancor that explodes
when the mistress shows at the funeral parlor,
when the strung out junkie steals his mother's rings,
whenever we realize *almost* only counts in horse shoes.

And no one plays horseshoes on my street.

In First Grade

In first grade, amid Lysol, eraser crumbs, and sweaty hands
Johnny Kazuba was forced to help me with my penmanship
which, according to Sister George, was seven circles of hell
lower than chicken scratch.
Johnny had a tiny nose pinched by enormous
maple syrup colored glasses. Everyone (the nuns
and cafeteria ladies) said he'd be a priest one day.
Twenty years later, he overdosed on smack but
for all I know, his penmanship was still intact.

"Just a spoonful of sugar helps the medicine go down,
the medicine go down, the medicine go down…"

Julie Andrews, according to Sister George, was a saint.
How else to explain that thrilling, bell pure voice?
My brother, an aficionado of sexual bliss in unlikely places,
claimed Julie had the most spectacular tits in all of Hollywood.
At six, neither tits nor sainthood wooed me.
I wanted to make perfect Catholic Palmer method P's and Q's.

"Edelweiss, edelweiss, every morning you greet me."

I dreamed Julie Andrews spun madly down the rows
where we were seated according to our "God-given IQ's,"
displaying her well bred yet spectacular English titties.
Johnny Kazuba was somber even then and whispered, "sorry"
as sister forced him to cup his hand on mine and guide me
over the paper I had torn, trying to write like normal children.

"Julie Andrews has an excellent Palmer children" Sister said,
"I have her autograph by way of conclusive evidence."

Johnny's damp, pudgy child's hand moved clasped with mine
in miserable synchronicity, making one large circle
entwining another—the spiral helix of failure,
two doomed figure skaters carving figure eights
in the ice of an unlined and merciless universe,
while the paper tore, and tore, was rent
like the curtain before the ark of the covenant,
My moron's tears splotched the page.

"I could have danced all night, I could have danced all night!"
And my shame already ancient by age six sang back:
"Fuck you, fuck you, fuck you."

In Another Life

Suffering builds character, she said.
I hadn't suffered yet, so I took her word for it.

I waited and the days passed.
A tit mouse in the thorny locust
could send me into transports.

Doing nothing never bored me.
I could watch the world until it disappeared
and all that remained was the intensity of my stare.

I watched how she drank one cup of black coffee, then another,
I watched her chain smoking chesterfield kings,
And the way she wept
when we couldn't pay the oil man
and for three days our family slept in the kitchen,
the stove on five hundred degrees.

I thought this communal sleep was the best of things,
all the people I loved
gathered in one place,
huddled under blankets,
warm in the stove's dark maw
with its one blue fang of flame.

I heard her in the middle of night.
What will we do?
And when grandma paid the bill,
and let her know her choice in men was suspect,
she cried some more
and I said: "you're a mean old witch"
to my grandmother
and my mother slapped me,
sent me reeling into the sofa.

And then I knew
this woman with the prettiest green eyes,
who seemed a goddess to me.
I knew what suffering did to her,
how it stole her eyes from the thorny locust,
made the tit mouse beside the point. "I hate you" I shouted.
"I wish you were dead,"
and she took me in her arms,
saying "shush, shush,"
and my grandmother stood there
sick of the melodrama.
"Don't baby that rude little boy.
That's his trouble.
You've spoiled him."

And I ran out of the house
and pressed my face against the locust thorns
until I bled,
And all that time my character was building,
building towards
her death at the age of fifty, and my father's death,
and the stubborn love of my eyes
that had no purpose but to stare.
And I remember this poem by Jimenez
and it is my poem
and it's my only revolution:
How I am like a child they
drag through the fiesta of the world,
my eyes cling madly to things,
and what misery when I am torn away.

Crayola Hymn

Forest green made me think of fishing shows,
and, later, when I'd matured out of that,
Sibelius, and Christ knows
I spent many a pretentious day
listening to Finlandia,
brooding on the northern lights,
and reading "Ozymandias."

I was a creep. Didn't copper disappoint
when my eyes only saw it as a duller gold?
And gold, too, seemed always out of joint,
especially when compared to periwinkle blue.

Ah periwinkle! I liked the name—
both mollusk and flower, and part of the band
of Crayola's deluxe set, singing synasthesias to the sky,
conducted by my plump, unartistic hand.

I knew the sounds of colors—
the deep purple violins,
and the corn flower blue—
a trumpet at midday,
when a jet scratched its mark
upon the afternoon,
and a monarch licked the salt
of a stone, then flew away.

If only now I could see as clear as then,
and let my seeing hear, my hearing see,
I'd return to some sense of truth beyond the sprawl
of all this maudlin "tragedy."

God grant me that confusion
of sound and sight and sense,
mandarin be your love,
dark blue your recompense.

Ethics for Huey O'Donnell

So a friend comes over and you hand him
six big squash, and a nice purple eggplant,
and three or four zucchini from your garden,

the soil still clinging to the fruit of your labors,
your hands still smooth and dirty,
and the friend has something to tell you:

He's got a rare and virulent cancer,
six months maybe to live,

and you give the *oh-my-God* look…"Huey!"
and you put your arms around him because, hey, that's what friends do,

but you feel nothing at that moment, nothing because cancer and virulent
and six months to live are just words, conceptual realities,

and the guy standing before you is tall and handsome
and wearing the same stupid cowboy belt you could never
get away with wearing, and he is going to die.

He doesn't look like someone who is going to die.
He looks like the guy women unintentionally hurt you with
by saying: "Do you think Huey might…"
He's the guy whose ass your own mother checked out,
and, for all your genuine affection for him,
you have often wished he was dead, or a little less blessed
with good looks and now he is going to die, and you feel
many official and unofficial things—none of which match,
but your greatest feeling at the moment is anger.

How can you tell me this when I have just given you
a big purple eggplant? This is what you would say, if you had no editor

between your mouth and your heart, and then you would
punch him, and knock his glasses off, and
smash the veggies in his hands, and really hug him—with all
the fear of a true friend, which you are—a true friend, but also a false

and the false wins right now because that's what he needs—

the one who will say the expected, ineffectual things, who will not
tell him what he already knows: how you envied him all of your life,
and part of you is glad he's the one who is dying, and not you,
and yet you love him, love him with all your lack of integrity—

like a big fucking eggplant still covered with dirt, with the stem
quivering like an umbilical—infantile, beyond the decorum
you now uphold, knowing that awkwardness, and platitudes,
and the fine art of "that sucks" is all he or you can handle,
the falsity—the loving falsity Cordelia could not manage.

Oh and how you hate that bitch, Cordelia, who was so virtuous, she couldn't
tell her father a single kiss ass lie.

There is a maw into which even the best feet dangle,
and we are fed to our deaths and why say the truth
now when you've been avoiding it all these years—
whatever it is, whatever it is, you're not sure,
except you love him, and feel nothing right now
and say: wait a minute…I forgot to give you

some tomatoes,
and trudge back out into the warm late summer light,
glad to flee for a moment, and it is only when he
takes one tomato in his hand, having put down the bounty
for a moment, and feels its heft, and juggles it
like a ball player waiting for a game, that you cry,
and, when you come to—rise up from the animal self,
you're in his arms, and he's telling you to chill. It's alright.
And it's not alright. And that's alright, too.

I Am What I Remember

The stolid, heavy lidded gaze
of a giant sea turtle
on whose back I rode when I was five
still troubles me in dreams,

though surrounded in memory
by the repossessed and garish
furniture of my uncle John:
an alcoholic diabetic
who died an hour before Repo-Men
could haul away his life.

On his lap lay a plate
of blue and cracked chintz,
and, on his spit-shined Oxfords,
a wedge of tuna sandwich.
For all his desperation he was
natty, clean, precise,
a man who calmly, and with little fuss,
assumed his death.

I am only what I remember:
the brief, peripheral touch
of a woman's hand
on my lower back
as she squeezed past me
in the seventh grade,
the scent of chalk dust and henna
her breasts pressed against my back
still troubling me in sleep,
the hand still sinking in.
And where does it end?
My uncle told me once
I could take my plastic shovel
and dig a hole all the way to China.

He was lying. Memory lies,
but its touch remains
inscrutable and sure
as the sound of an old Victrola
softly hissing behind a voice,
until it becomes half the tune.

The turtle rises slowly,
his long neck strains
forth from the shell, stretches
until the tendons seem
on the verge of snap,
and my father says:
Joseph, smile for chrissakes.
And my mother pleads:
*Come on sweetie, look up at
the camera,* as I begin to wail.

Somehow knowing this turtle and me
are in deep shit, that this horror,
this crucifixion is no fun day at the zoo.
I am the turtle's cry.

And I hear the tired voice
of the photographer, a three inch
ash on his stogy, remark:
A bit touchy, ain't he?
And the camera flashes,

that picture lost six houses ago,
a life time re-possessed.

How heavy the lids of the turtle,
and of my uncle, and now mine—

with sleep or its absence?
What can you do?

The furniture waits to be lifted,
the props of a life carried off
and to where? I don't know.

Slowly, in the merciless
light of the flash,
the turtle blinks, and,
rising on his limbs, eyes hooded,
begins to crawl.

The Fat Lady Looks at Monet

Summer heat rash
between her legs,
thighs chafing
under her dress,
she enters the Monet room
to stare at his Water Lilies.

No one has touched her in years
except by accident.

The lilies bloom from their blue
world—red and white.

She dreams their thick roots
anchor deep in the mud of her life,
cold, and concealed.

She is weightless there,
her body a blue desire, moving
with a sort of sacred ease, equal in beauty
to the river grass.

Sway, sway, she is eyes half closed and sway.
A couple steps in front of her,
obscuring her view.

Excuse me she says.
They turn and stare.

Sweat dries on her breast bone,
trickles down her back.
She closes her eyes fully,
imagines that pond.

From the bank, salamanders scoot,
a heron's shadow flies,
and a gold carp rises to snatch the misery
from her outstretched hands.

The Girl from Ipanema

There were gerbils in her living room,
roaming freely about, ambushing my sneakers
from a scattered New York Times.
Ah but she had comic book black hair,
plush, and thick, and so black that it was blue.
"I'll put them in their cage," she said, determined,
searching for their home amid
the discarded athletic bras,
and cartons of dried out Lo Mein.
"I can't find it," she said, winsome,
forlorn, brushing back her epic mane.
A high heel without its match,
dangled like a shot bird from her hand.

I helped search (I am a helpful guy).
I lunged (I am that guy, too),
wanting to replace the awkwardness
of the moment with
the awkwardness of the moment.

Our tongues had a good long talk.
The high heel fell from her hand.
Meanwhile, this heel was hard and eager to ignore
the gerbils scampering over our feet.

An hour later, after we had cleared
a path to her bed, and tripped on the cage
she said: "I'm not very neat."
I said: "That's alright,"
lust being the most forgiving of inspectors.
In lieu of clean glasses, we swigged
Shiraz from the same bottle.
I hate Shiraz! I hate the sound
of scuttling rodents, but her hair
was comic book black, and her tongue
could say yes in fifty languages.
Come morning, the sun slanted in
on a squalor so vast it was almost

stylish: ash trays overflowing, beer bottles
that subbed for ash trays, pizza boxes,
their contents petrified,
dust on all the photos except those
of some former boyfriend from Brazil.
(Sugar Loaf Mountain rose behind him.)
His lats were ashimmer in perpetual sun,
his long, lean body, his perfect brown
made me feel like a beached Albino.

In one photo he stood, relaxed, smiling,
some impossibly beautiful child holding his hand,
a stuffed panda clutched to her chest, and
there too, the object of my desire,
wearing a floppy hat, nose freckled,
eyes shaded from the glare.
It was the only thing dusted in that apartment,
there on her night table, the glass free of smudges,
the frame an ornate gold.

I might have felt ashamed if I'd been a
'sensitive' man,
but instead, I snuck out of bed,
feet tentative, unsure of what they'd touch,
hearing her murmur and roll, the smell of
wine souring the air,
and I said a prayer to Saint Anthony
to find my socks, my belt, my pants.
Then walking carefully to the kitchen,
watched by the gerbils up on their hinds,
their little Simon Legree paws suspended
in mid air, I found a broom, and began
sweeping a path to the dishes,
like the wind in Joyce's poem,
whistling merrily all the while
around her despair.

43

II. How Holy

For My Lord, Jesus Christ

Were you not alive to the last moment
and, for this reason, your death was not

unbearable to me? Was that the courage you offered?
Or perhaps I broke at the pure sound of your tolling.

I don't know if I am dead or alive.
This is the gift you gave—
removing every cheap certainty,
forcing me to walk on water.

The ground refuses any longer
to keep up appearances. It
swallows the feet that stand,
that still keep their pact with
ground.

Ground is not ground. It is
the waves I always feared.

And why fear them?
Did you not say: grass, stone, tree
until they said: Thou?

At the sound of Thou,
the cheapest whore was Christ.

I touch your five wounds
to touch my own. Have mercy on me

who is still so afraid of drowning.

Have mercy on me, who believes the lie
of death.
Let me call out your name
until your name calls me.

Let me say: grass, stone, tree,
until I am spoken.

Prayer

In what cannot be fixed

made whole again

in what will not suffice

the inadequate thing, the broken body

in this, oh Lord, my God,

in this,

my heart like a box of

defective watches,

my ego the size of Maine,

my anger, and loss, and lust,

in this please come, abide,

sit with me at the table of my sins

and breathe Your Word.

Remembrance

We'd all try for Father Reardon.
He'd thumb the ashes deep.
Black crosses on our foreheads,
we proceeded out of church,
giggling, poking each other,
ashes to ashes, dust to dust,
into the brilliant sunlit noon
that made us squint.

Now where am I who feels no mark of belonging?
It was comforting to know we were
all going to die someday—the popular and the shunned;
all of us equal, in the community of ashes.

Now where? Often,
I hear the high, shrill voices of children
playing in some distance.
There is always one voice louder, shriller
than the rest.
It cuts through my life and makes its dark incision.
It is like the thumb of Father Reardon,
pressing home the Word.

From One Hundred Variations on a Relationship to God

The care with which I unravel
so that no one notices
until there is hardly anything left
but this spool,

and the slow loss
of ambitions—major or minor,

and one day perhaps
all I want to do is
lift myself into the trees

and disappear—

like some semi-colon who grew tired
of keeping separate but related sentences together.

Do you understand?

I am lifting what can not be supported,
the gods enjoy the sound of cracking bones,

and why should I disappoint them?

Ruins look good in the grass
provided they are not trying to get up,
not trying to continue—

like that fighter I saw punched
into the canvas, who thought it was heroic
to twitch and stagger upright,
or that woman who wrapped the blankets
tighter around her dead infant, as if futility

could call forth a resurrection.

Nothing works, and it is an abomination and
the gods can suck my dick, I obey

only to annihilate you—to say with the breaking,

I spit out my teeth against you , and my blood on your pure white gowns,

here, where defiance is the only torture,
the only consolation,

to raise my face to your stupid, all powerful
insipid fists, until you grow tired,
and, out of boredom, let me drop.

Haiku Salt Mines

The past
and all its adjectives.
This snow covered log. This wet ass.

Copper pots
hung from a loose nail.
Everything, getting ready to fall.

The engine seized.
The check bounced.
Danced in the snow covered parking lot.

Many years ago
granmah dipping a spoon
into a soft boiled egg.

One rabbit.
One evil landlord.
A single bullet.

Sweet gum leaves,
red, black, yellow, orange,
why sweep them up?

Satin sheets.
Attempting to fuck,
the knees slip.

The glass dolphin
struck by one more snow flake
shatters.

Singing into a fan,
Summer, voice
chopped—ten fingers of sound.

In a car,
my hand on your knee
my brain somewhere else.

Atop the flood wall
a single dandelion
and an enormous used condom.

Picking blackberries
until against the bucket
not a sound.

Dean Martin on YouTube.
Outside, a thousand stars.
Somewhere between them.

Watching an old
Hercules movie, mouth moving
long after the words are said.

Me Ma died. Me Dad Died.
All aunts, all uncles dead
This piss is for them!

Taking a piss in the sea.
Pitch dark vital boom
of unseen waves.

Roar family! Trickle in
ye bastards! White glow
of my sneakers.

The apple orchards
in bloom. A white fire
in the moonless fields.

Shopping cart in river.
Ice along its edge,
muskrat slithers out.

The way she kissed me—
holding her hair from her face
not even trying.

More Haiku

Under the faucet
her black hair
more flowing water.

The small stain
on a couch in a room
too clean for stains.

A hole in my sock.
Painting a face on my toe,
wiggling it, you laugh.

Locust trees on campus.
Some thorns five inches long.
No one sees.

Catfish,
horned fin bloodied
punctuates my thumb.

Moonlight.
The sheen of fish slime
on my hands.

Reeling in
a four foot eel.
still writhing in the pan.

Dog licking the other dog's
balls. Two well dressed ladies
hold leashes, chat.

Roof rain.
Having just fucked,
you teach me how to hold chop sticks.

Roof rain insomnia.
Two years after we broke up.
the hardness of your nipples.

Poem for Advent

The world takes us at its leisure
slowly, by increments of infamy
or "virtue"

and beyond that taking
we wager freedom
against our corpses,
trick ourselves into living

fully—whatever fully means.
I am writing this in the dust
of an old Chrysler,
its lascivious grill, its chrome
freckled with rust,

its front end grinning
like Burt Lancaster
in Elmer Gantry.

What do I mean?

A million dollar grin,
the atavistic power of healthy teeth

might convert a nation (see Joel Osteen),
might make us believe in
the power of "abundance."

But suppose I write:

"Lack is the necessity of being."

The nation will turn against me.

The sun is a used car salesman.
To get something for almost nothing
is the pitch of grifters and of angels.
And I have been both
con and evangelist.

"Fear not" says Gabriel,
the usual line
(See Britannica, 1962: how an angel gets one foot in the door)
"For the Lord of Lords has chosen you."

And the little girl inside us nods her head.

"Yes."

The birds cheep.
Bird twitter and angelic hosts are all around us.

I am postponing the inevitable
until further notice.

Pregnant with God,
I write in the dust of an old Chrysler,
all the sins of the ones with stones.

Slowly they turn away,
and I am left with the woman
taken in adultery,
and I am left with my own
trembling girl, who kneels
in the deepest part of my sarcasm,

beyond all cons, who cries

Maranatha! Who waits
that the spirit might shadow her,
that the womb might not be empty,
that, even in despair, the soul might
feel its worth, and , feeling it,
despair more deeply into joy—this dark thing
that comes to save us from our "truths"

this dark season where poverty is blessed.

Practicing Betrayal

This round thing that finds only squares
in a world where roundness is preached,
how does it live?
Does it cut itself into corners?
Does it cube its lies?

At eight, I was encouraged
to dive in the filthy river.
All my friends stood at the shore,
promising they'd go next.
As soon as my head bobbed up,
I heard their laughter,
my eyes level with their sneakers,
dripping sewage, I could smell
their contempt.
They called me shit-boy for a year.

And the neighborhood, with its indolence,
its comfortable poverty: just when
I was stepping into it, it collapsed:
drugs, cancer, layoffs,
the neighbors changing hues, changing shape,
in infinite flight, even the houses
gone from hopeful patches of grass
and Virgin Marys to
shattered glass, and foreclosure signs.

I believe in the next banana peel,
the rug pulled out.

I am in the river before they even ask,
diving down as deep as possible.
How long will they stand at the shore,
waiting to call me stupid?
Instead I claim this destruction,
make it something I can count on.
I square the moon.
Misfit it into place.
This is my way
to live—
dive deep
until
the round has
found an edge
and I am
the only
traitor left.

Refusing the Sea

for Adam Fitzgerald

White crested, the green waves wallop you
though you stand gull stoic and watch them foam,
and hardly blink, as if a pair of wax wings
grew from your back, and you rose to fit the air,
vagrant, and at ease, your long hair riffling every wind,
blue fired bright, drawn out from the kiln of the sun.

And what is this oppressive heaviness
towards which you pit the gravity of your stare?
How long will it hold you? This shore
line turns and shifts, the pebbles grabbed from under you
by the magician sea, a tablecloth
from which the glass days are upended,
until you're the only thing left standing,
alone, so fiercely alone, utterly
content to spoil the tricks of the sea
which wants only to make you weightless in its arms,
wants only what you want, and you refuse.

Vesper

At night, when the piano becomes a bird
and glides over the gas company building,
I sink my fingers into keys,
playing the sore back and tired eyes
of my beloved.
And who's to say this music isn't real?
From the edge-lit reeds of rivers,
from the shadows of undercut banks,
one dark consoling voice
swims out, abandoning its lair.
All over the earth, there's
the long wake of things in passing,
and the ghost of an egret
folding her ancient wings.

I Have Come at Last to This Circle of Shadows

I have come, at last, to this circle of shadows,
shadows whose ward and wean I be,
be it tongued forth or as mute as snow,
snow shaken forth from the black thorn tree,

I have come to this circle and have labored,
labored at what I did not know
knowing only I labored, and now must rest,
rest in the black thorn upon the snow.

Things I Want to Do Before I Die

I want to curl up in a slightly dark and
leathery library—naked—on a cold marble floor
in the fetal position
and remove from her feet slowly, with great reverence,
the spiked high heels of Sophia Loren.
I want to talk intelligently,
and at length,
about olive oil, it's history and tradition,
the light on the olive groves at, say, two o'clock
when siesta is nearly over, and I am awakened
from a nap in the arms of the olive master's daughter.
I want to know how to braid hair.
I want to whistle for a cab. I have never done so,
nor have I lit a match off my shoe, nor have I
stood in a vast wheat field at dusk in Idaho,
squinting towards the horizon, in the full knowledge
that I am the "heart" of America, and may even be
its next president.
I want a statue of me erected right next to Balzac
in the courtyard of MOMA
and I want to see a cardinal light
on my bronze dome as the snow falls and various
high fashion models sit in rapt silence, admiring my likeness.
In lieu of all this, I would like to look both elegant and eloquent
for just one hour—my shoes shined, shirt tucked
everything in place, and sing the Agnus Die perfectly
while one yellow leaf fell from the eighty foot
gingko tree in the Episcopalian
graveyard on Broad Street in Elizabeth
where I used to sit for hours reading
when I was a boy and didn't think of death.

III. IT'S LIKE THIS

Improvisation on a Theme by Auden

Poetry makes nothing happen
and thank God,
I like the barely swaying
golden rod
firmly entrenched, its roots in that black soil
bee humped, this golden ragamuffin weed
that grows all golden, and has gone to seed.

Listen: Hear the last bee of the year,
deep in the pollened fur, its slender legs
glutted with what makes the bear suspend
five hundred pounds of self to swat the hive,
what would we not do to stay alive
for something sweet?
for something worth
the sting?
She called me names, she called me not at all,
and I rose up and swung my claws. The air
was not impressed. It didn't feel a thing,
the hive was in the mind, not in that tree
against the air, bear like an angry bee
swung deep into its sorrow and its rage,
tore nothing, was paid nothing as its wage
What good's desire if it doesn't win?
Go ask the bear, he labored, he should know.
The golden rod nods to what winds might blow
beyond the getting and the almost got,
it keeps a still, and unassuming spot
upon my hill, does nothing, rides the breeze,
and, in the fall, makes horny lovers sneeze.

Clap Out Love's Syllables

Clap out love's syllables. Stock markets fall.
The gravity of apples and of gold
have nothing on the way our bodies sprawl
and touch the accent of what we two now hold
both tensed and tendered. Touching, we disdain
all commerce, and all wantonness seems blessed.
We grope and cop at leisure, we remain
stable in our instability.
And this is good, and this is good, we kiss
all nipple and thigh pleasured, we descend
to where no share, no bonding gone amiss
can cheat us of a happy dividend.

Stocks fall, leaves fall, we fall, yet, falling, praise
the fields of lust on which our bodies graze.

Reunion

Your hair like liquid amber struck by light
has lost its luster, and your full soft lips
have thinned to tidy scars, as, standing tight
mouthed, livid with hello, your right hand grips
a bag from Lord and Taylor's. You've suppressed
the urge to kill your children. You have made
a pact with "nice." I remember you undressed
and vagrant in my arms. What price we've paid
for being "happy" in the common way,
for our civility, for pleasing those
who only wanted all things gone astray
to march in step, towards what? God only knows.

But we have learned, and learning, we remain
cordial, phatic, dead in our disdain.

Why I Hate Tercets (An Essay on My Aesthetics)

My ex-lover always wrote in tercets,
so, too, my poet/cardiologist,
neat, little three toed

sheep, without blemish, without stain,
benign, the sort of bucolic verse
professors snore to in summer.

I admit that I'm a slob,
that I have never seen a tercet
my sprawl could really live in.

Something is wrong with me, no doubt,
something broken that fails
to adjust to the tidy symmetry of

"A life more sanely lived."
Don't get me wrong. I donate to Green Peace.
I am not immune to desire.

Outside, the trees keep swaying
strange things to me,
little green words like:

"Kelp!" But I'm unable to rise
beyond my own shapelessness to
where I hear the squeaky clean windows

begging the leaves for a scratch.
They are so lonely, they want only to be touched.
They are tired of being clean.

Me, too! My fingers smudge their glass.
This is a mission of mercy. Let it be so.
This is an act of grace.

The trees, the windows, and I
will have to find something
better to do with our lives,

something beyond tripping
over antique furniture, stumbling
through a series of orderly rooms

which have become too tasteful,
too stilted, too small
for anyone's good.

Poet as a Young Voyeur

The little blue house
with its cedar bark shingles,
and the little tree
a miserable sterile pear,
and the little old lady
with the yapping schnauzer,
stopping to berate
her perfectly bald husband,
and the husband swinging
his garden hose violently
in futile protest
as she goes inside—
as if he were mowing down
house tree wife
with a Thompson sub
and all of it seen by the poet
as he sits in the tree house,
eight years old, crew cut,
having grown tired
of the big breasted cleavage
in the Vampire comics

and then Venus rises, evening star
over the billboard of the Marlboro man,
horse cantering through snow drifts,
a cigarette dangling
from his tight lipped and determined mouth,
and he looks up at the planet
a bright white-blue
in the gloaming
and notices the bald man
is looking, too,
as if his real life
were there
where a jet climbs
out of Newark Airport
into the approaching dark
that swallows them whole

I Love You, Ruin My Life

Hey hat! Hey jaunty angle,
hey crooked nose, ear spangle,
hey hot then cold, you young, me old,
come here, as bold as light,
and tongue me gentle and all erudite—
till skin be wise, and dazzled as white spray
on dark arched hump of waves. In essence: stay
and bid me love you, lose you, find you here
like coins, like pens beneath couch cushions. Spare
me no pain, nor pleasure, nor surprise
beside, inside you, hey hat, hey love, hey, rise!

Poem in Which the Ghost of Andrew Marvell Returns as a Greaser to Plight His Immortal Troth

Now that we have outlawed time
and the duck asses of yesteryear
reappear at dusk, in the frail light of
telephone booths, singing "Gloria"
to the stars,
will you go out with me?

All of history is a vain attempt
to rig the answer to this question.
We could pretend we fight for social justice,
and no courtship is complete without
such pretense, but darlin', you know just what I'm here for.
And doesn't that make sense?

It's late. Rain pelts the glass ghosts
of telephone booths. I have one dime left,
with the profile of Wallace Steven's wife
imposed upon its flip side.
And your silhouette's on the shade!

I have sung "Teen Angel," in the highest falsetto.
I have sung "Little Darlin'" in the heart of the ghetto.
I have raised the dead.
What more could a girl want? I promise you
the moon with complementary dishes,
a heaven tree of stars with all your favorite wishes,
come true!
Oh you, oh you, oh you!

Peeling back the crinoline,
twelve layers of suspended rapture,
will I find the corpse of your evil twin?
In spite of such fears,
I have not tired of my desire to win!
I would have you under the false palms
of a thousand cheesy night clubs.
I would have you in New Mexico beside
the skull of Georgia O'Keeffe.
I would have you, or come to grief!

"Sloppy seconds!" cries the sparrow.
I admit my politics are narrow,
and I am in bad need of a trim.
But must you go out with—with him?

God forbid such incredulity!
Come on darlin', come and go with me!
And we shall haunt the gutted bowling alleys
of the lost American dream, shouting:
"Vitalis!" our favorite word in Latin,
for our eyes are pools of stars,
and our lips are the finest satin.
And why should you say no
and forsake the soft sibilant of yes?
My finger is sliding towards second base.
A cloud of sand dust swirls about!
Oh umpire of my heart!
Don't cry: "Out!"

I Was a Cougar Hunter

The old man in the auto repair shop
where I am busy waiting for a car
that can't be fixed
tells me he was a cougar hunter

out west, he says, he's a Chickasaw.

And he never shakes my hand
or says hello, but begins:

I was cougar hunter.

Why should I doubt it? The creases in his face
are ravines, and the eyes scratch their
blue flint to my face,
until I ignite and become
the small fire that knows his voice:

Yep, hunted 'em in the Dakotas.

He claims there were pretty girls
in Bismarck, big Swedish girls, but they all got fat.

Ain't that the way?

His wife was pretty. Now she's dead.
Good woman. Never gave him a bit of trouble.

There's cougar here, you know,
he tells me, they're coming back.

He can feel out a cat, he says, they're here.

And I believe him. I believe the cougars
are here even now in these hills,
bringing down the deer, waiting out
the groundhogs in their dens.

He goes out to his car
to fetch a walleye lure.
See them teeth marks?
Been a lot of wallys in my life.

When he leaves, my friend asks
why the nut jobs always talk to me.

I am seeing a cougar stalk
through drifts of snow.
I don't know.

Break Up Poem

I need the waste—
a field where snow falls, where there is
no beloved telling me all the
reasons I can no longer matter
in that same grave voice
a judge uses to sentence men to death:

Gravitas, gravitas, Oh fuck it all.
No solemn executions!

Beyond my need to touch
that which was never
truly—
I committed no crime

except desire.

I wanted, I wanted, I wanted—

but now this field
is dark, the snow
not yet covering the grass
falls, and fails,
and does not cease to fall—

the things of this world are true.
Love must be a thing or a lie
and she was never snow.

Cautionary Tale (Or Variations on the Theme of Malevolence)

Watching a swan trip over the knot of an oak root,
I was delighted.
It was like witnessing the fall from grace
of a particularly austere and "virtuous" politician,
like watching the pretty figure skater collapse
in mid triple axle double camel spin—
and she did not cry!
And the crowd loved her because failure
at such a high level is God-like, awesome
a purging of their far less than spectacular pratfalls.
In her case it was worth six million dollars more
in endorsements than if she had won the gold.
So I might advise you to fail at the levels of Swans
and stars. Yes. I could attempt that cheap moral.
But the Swan was beautiful and after a second of
complete un-swan like behavior
She preened herself, ruffled her feathers
then descended again into the waters
of the polluted and un-swan like Rahway river,
her white body soiled green with algae, her
dignity intact, except that now I hated her.
Perhaps I had always hated her. But now my
hatred felt lofty—a contempt so vast
so high and mighty that I no
longer noticed Swans, though others might
point them out, shout: "Look!"
I kept my chin up, my eyes forward,
in search of the knottiest roots.

Checkmate

There will be no more good days
even if you pray your rosary
and quit smoking,
and give up booze and sex,

the world will have just enough sympathy
to make itself but never you feel good.

You may as well keep tight lipped.
(They'll mistake it for nobility.)

There will no longer be good days
and there never was
a reason except maybe some
hidden test you failed,
some gene you inherited,
some corner of the universe
that you happened to sleep in
where all the shit piled up.

Now the things you liked
to eat make you sick,
and being brave, or upbeat
or negative
makes you sick. No one
wants to touch you
if they can avoid it
without looking callous,
and some don't even
mind looking callous,
(and you are grateful for them),

but that dead leaf,
that dead thing you
see floating
on the swift current
of a half iced over stream—

that somehow still delights you,
watch it then.

When all the assholes of
uplift come
to make a philosophy, a
value out of it
hurt them— scratch out their eyes,
spit in their faces,
tell them to take their
bogus spiritual comforts and go home,

and don't ask why, don't ask why
it should do more for you
than padre pio
or all the asshole saints.

It does. It delights you.
It isn't nature. Fuck nature.

It's just a dead leaf
heading down a steel gray
muscled stream

so swift, too violent, ever
to freeze over.

Keep your eye on it.
Walk away
when it has given you
all that it can, more than friends,
or the hundred
teachers of the law,
the liars of why
can ever give.

Let it help you
live another hour,
another day,
not because life is sacred, or holy
or worthwhile, but because,
just because, just because
it is—

Dandelions

Gone to seed gone to
gosling, old lady fuzz,
gone from the bright
yellow,
gone things—ugly stalk
and spores I kick

with my work boot
to watch the seeds
explode—the violence

with which I kick the dandelions,
the tenacious, imperturbable
bane of lawn love.

I love no lawn. I love
these wasted, little hags
I kick.

They are mine. They are mine:
they are the old bitches
at 6 o'clock mass

who always and never die,
someone's grandma I hoist
on the steel toe of my boot.

I kick her to the moon.
She cries: *touch me.*
The things of this world

cry, *touch me.* The things
of this world cry,
dandelion.

Dead Things

That rooster I found on the
tenth floor of the Fairmount Luxury Apartments,
just wandering around in the hall,
Rhode Island Red, fierce,
and coming towards me with his spurs...

How did he get there?

Or the time I was struck in the back of the head
by a pineapple that had somehow
been catapulted from a truck,
and I woke ten minutes later,
with a beautiful Egyptian woman
leaning over me,
her breath smelling miraculously
of coconuts, the intense sadness of her eyes,
not for me, but for every humiliated
and haphazard thing:

What is it?
And how do I know she was Egyptian?

I must have asked her, or perhaps misremembering
is a form of prayer.

What have I not misremembered
so that even your hand, beloved,
resting on mine, now,
and tracing the pale blue vein
just below the knuckle
dissolves into a vast mistake,

a fen of almost-theres
that are never just so
just so this hour of being real—

the cup, the long ago voices
of family,
the sobs I hear come out from my own throat—

this animal that walks away from inside me,
this thing I have sought to kill,

my spurs slicing the air, my crown
of feathers bristling as I rage,
my life out of place, and not

my life at all.

Widower

When he can't stand the ripe clusters of grapes next door,
or the next door neighbor attending to his vines,
or the way sunlight dapples the neighbor's eye glasses,
and falls, with the shadows of leaves, on the neighbor's wife's good legs,

he thinks how something has happened to him,
a great tree gone down in the self—
and it will not rise up, but is this sorry mess
of exposed roots, and rotted wood.

Then disgust dries the spit in his mouth, and he tells his neighbor
to keep that goddamned dog off his property, or he'll shoot it,
and goes inside the house, pulling down all the shades,
and, opening the closet, he takes out her blue dress and red cloth coat,
the one with the over sized gold buttons, and sits
for a long time, shades drawn, smoothing them with his hands.

Why Quitting Feels Like Love

Perhaps it is
this admission
finally
that nothing may succeed or
push
through the sameness
of a life except

this giving up
this tendering
one's resignation
this walking out
of it only
more so, a
landscape complete with
shadows of possibility
which no effort
however arduous
can achieve:

a newness
in the east!
a vermillioned somethingness
of which we are too
distantly a part
in "I quit," "That's it"
"fuck you!"

How much like love it seems
how much
these first few steps
out of something into
what?

Wanting to Lick the Instep of Your Foot While You Read Larry Levis

I want to lick the instep of your foot
when you put on your reading glasses,
and, sitting primly propped on both feet,
read me a poem.

There are a thousand desires,
peripheral lusts that, if mentioned,
would ruin my sterling reputation.

Yes. Larry Levis is certainly a great poet.
But what would Larry do?

I imagine Elizabeth Bishop
going down on her South American lover,
the crazy one, who killed herself
in Bishop's Manhattan digs.

Bishop wrote "One Art" about that loss.
It does not mention
the taste of another woman.
Nothing is less memorable or portable
than sex, which is why we keep having it,
hoping it will stick this time—
why it is always new, if we count
not just the act itself, but all the
little acts that make us yearn for
something beyond whatever it is
we are currently pretending to do.
I kiss the hands that hold the book
and you swat me away, wanting me to listen.
I want to listen. I do.
Larry Levis is certainly a great poet.

But what would Larry do?
Elizabeth Bishop found the body
and composed a villanelle.
Disaster and lust must be bound
like Isaac to the rock.
They must be given shape.
The knife poised to strike,
and what God calls time out,
and sends an angel to
withhold the willing hand?

Mercy is a matter of suspension.
Suspended, I will my ears to hear.
This poem is important to you.
It is by Larry Levis.
It makes the hairs stand up
on your slender arms.

But, if one foot comes out
from under your ass, I swear
I will grab it, and hold it in my hands.
Because I like you better than Larry Levis.
That's why I'm listening.
That's why I pretend to hear.

Dignity

The dog, a yellow lab,
was lying in the street
freshly hit by

a green Oldsmobile
driven by some old lady
who wept

as the crowd gathered
and the kid who owned the dog
ran over

to kneel in the street
to pet him while he
panted, his coat

smeared with blood, his
eyes wild with pain
and yet he licked her face—

the salt of her tears,
and she stroked his head
until the cops showed up

with everyone gathered around
the dying animal
except the old lady

who spoke no English,
who looked like
she might pass out

in a black coat,
her pocket book
clutched to her chest

removed from the innocent,
her white hair glowing
red in the siren light.

And I put my arm around
her—the murderer
who smelled of peppermints

and whiskey.

Whatever the Heart was Given to Chew

I once wanted a life in which my biggest problem
was a cheaper way to caulk the windows:
I wanted a sliding glass door that looked out
on Portuguese tiles, and an aqua pool,
and a friend or two to support
as long as they didn't lean too heavily
upon me.
I wanted a lawn with a well lit sprinkler system
and, when the occasional bad and young
and pretty girl frolicked in its well lit splendor,
and wet her halter so that her nipples
stood erect, I wanted a fine and nuanced
discontent, a brief sigh, a sadness like early autumn
to fall on my well aged, but fully functioning cock.

And I would go into the house and fuck
my middle aged, but well preserved wife
in a way I hadn't fucked in years,
gripping the bed board till my knuckles
paled, slamming her into bliss.

Normal is as normal does.
The feeble pulse of happiness
is the only pulse I ever wanted to take.

Instead, I was homeless,
And the twitter of birds made me angry
and I lost my heart and my teeth,
and no longer know the difference.
What is a heart?
The yellow light
from other people's houses
takes me in its jaws. Satan has nothing

on the suburbs. Now
I would settle for a different
flavor of sadness—one more bland,
more chewable, easier to spit out
on those who never claimed me.
The grass is bending in the wrong direction.
The wind must feel venial.
A sudden interest in Jesus won't work.
To a man acquainted with suffering,
numbness becomes a balm, and embalmed
he walks carefully over the same terrain
thinking it will somehow be different,
somehow it will be alright if he takes just
the right amount of steps, a sort of spell
he knows all the words to, but can not
utter—as if the child in him,
the one he has murdered, will rise from the dead,
and everything will be forgiven,
everything—as if the heart could grow teeth
and swallow whatever it was given to chew.

Villain

At the last second, poetry saves you,
undoing the knots of the dastardly villain
who has tied you to the tracks of your life,

leaving you striped with rail ties,
like a Salisbury steak
and with rope burns no less,
your voice gone husky with: "Help."

And who has heard you, small, breathy
reed that you are? Who has made out
thy singular desperate trill in the whirling Dervish
of the maelstrom?
What villanelle, what Roundelay, what barbaric yawp
might suffice to hatchet the ice round your heart,
and bid you: "Live! Live!! in a tremolo
surpassing all mandolins?
And you rise—both Penelope and Frankenstein,
to swallow what would have swallowed you.

Yes, it's alive, its alive! Whatever does the trick,

like a lover who knows exactly when to squeeze, and when
to refrain
from squeezing, whose hands roam you
like a happy mountaineer, knowing every hill,
every valley and shadow, the scent of your pines,
the secret places where the black truffle grows…

And so on and so forth—
the poem comes, at the last possible instant

as the train blows its mighty horn,
and the black coal clouds rise,
and you are so sure you are going to be
a thousand disparate pieces of self
spread for miles across the Penn central,
your teeth amid the chicory and jewel weed,
thy limbs shredded and hanging like moss
from the Queens Anne's lace,

but then the sure fingers, the calm basso profundo
declaring: I shall untie thee, fair one!
And you are swept up in its arms
and carried away, to a cabin in the woods,
and fed nectar, until the next episode
when, smug, and content, and thinking
the danger is past, you go back
to your careless and hum drum life,
buying and selling, giving and taking in marriage,
unaware, unaware that we are always tied to the tracks,
that the train is always approaching,
that "help" has a limitless number of variants,
that the poem comes to do
what can not be done, to save us from a death
we did not know we were dying,
a death we realize only after its sure hands
have done the deed.

Filthy River

I live near a filthy river.
I have always lived near a filthy river,
and yet the nymphs climb the metal netting
of half submerged shopping carts to sing to me!

What do they sing? Sometimes it's Palestrina,
and sometimes its Marvin Gaye.
Often I tie myself to the mast of a ship,
so as to be seduced but not
led away
into death. Occasionally,
I listen and drown.

I drown in a filthy river.
I have always drowned in a filthy river
to rise like Osiris with the dawn,
to sink in the mud that I know
is the source of all song.

I would ask you to join me,
but you swat your arms
and complain about the mosquitoes.

Let them bite, draw blood.
You will remember a song
from your childhood
or the first good kiss, or the way
light played on your legs the first time
you knew they were pretty.
Don't be afraid. I have made this poem
for you to enter. Enter the river.

The mud between your toes
is your mother. The sun on your freckled back
knows your name.
Willow thy hair, and roots thy limbs.
Climb the netting of half submerged shopping carts.
Sing Palestrina or Marvin Gaye. Sing in the river
until only the song remains.

About the Author

Joe Weil was born and raised in Elizabeth, New Jersey where he attended St. Mary of the Assumption grade school and high school. For over 20 years, Weil worked on the graveyard shift at various factories, mainly at National Tool and Manufacturing in Kenilworth, New Jersey. During this time, he became involved in hosting poetry readings in both New Jersey and New York, and founded the literary magazine *Black Swan Review*. Weil is currently a lecturer in the Creative Writing Department at Binghamton University. He has two other books of poetry: *Painting the Christmas Trees* (Texas Review Press) and *What Remains* (Night Shade Press).

About NYQ Books™

NYQ Books™ was established in 2009 as an imprint of The New York Quarterly Foundation, Inc. Its mission is to augment the *New York Quarterly* poetry magazine by providing an additional venue for poets already published in the magazine. A lifelong dream of NYQ's founding editor, William Packard, NYQ Books™ has been made possible by both growing foundation support and new technology that was not available during William Packard's lifetime. We are proud to present these books to you and hope that you will continue to support The New York Quarterly Foundation, Inc. and our poets and that you will enjoy these other titles from NYQ Books™:

Amanda J. Bradley	*Hints and Allegations*
Joanna Crispi	*Soldier in the Grass*
Ira Joe Fisher	*Songs from an Earlier Century*
Ted Jonathan	*Bones and Jokes*
Fred Yannantuono	*A Boilermaker for the Lady*
Grace Zabriskie	*Poems*

Please visit our website for these and other titles:

www.nyqbooks.org

CPSIA information can be obtained at www.ICGtesting.com
Printed in the USA
BVOW010709201112

305970BV00001B/11/P

9 781935 520108